D1565779

WINDOWPANES

WINDOWPANES

ELIZABETH WILSON

HEADMISTRESS PRESS

ISBN 9978-1-7358236-7-6

Cover art: photo of Violet Trefusis. Photographer, date, copyright
unknown. Thanks to Rita Mae Reese for colorizing the photo.
Cover & book design by Mary Meriam.

PUBLISHER
Headmistress Press
60 Shipview Lane
Sequim, WA 98382
Telephone: 917-428-8312
Email: headmistresspress@gmail.com
Website: headmistresspress.blogspot.com

Dedicated to the late Jason Shinder, poet, teacher, friend, and founder of the YMCA National Writers Voice program.

CONTENTS

Prayer for Windows

Do not long for transparency.
You may cause the death of birds,
startled by a solid sky.

UPPER LEFT

I Want to Kiss Her While She Is Still a Stranger

My teeth clamp
steadily. My mouth
dries instantly.
I abandon myself.
I begin small
acts of covering.
My cupped hand hovers
over my mouth when I
talk   eat   laugh.
I don't move to kiss her.
I practice saying goodnight.
My lips part, small
gestures of leaving.

Your Sister Brings Me an Orchard

Each day after class we sit
on steps together and she pulls

apples from her purple backpack.
We talk about impact, the body

in relation to space in relation to
the body. Or the body in relation

to itself. The body in relation
to another body. I talk circles

like rings inside a tree, suggesting
growth, but I'm going nowhere.

I suggest things. I don't indicate
my need directly. I am more

ashamed than afraid of judgment.
I think about baptism. I would drown

for you. I would deny
my body to protect you.

I crouch, walk with bad posture
because I am afraid of taking

too much space. I'm afraid
my body will speak ahead of me.

Nights I sleep with you
I bend and crease myself

into the sheets the way I cover
this paper with my hand.

SCALES

My finger scales the page
sideways. Even now,
my eyes can't decide

where to settle. I followed
the fish, those inky interruptions,
swimming in the sea of negative

space. I fell behind the school
somewhere between Sigma
and Theta waves.

You scooped me up,
held me in the bowl
you made with your hands.

MY LOVE

So small when you hold it
in your hands. My fingers
tighten, signing each
slow letter in your palm.
I understand this gesture:
your fist opens, then squeezes
closed in your sleep.

PHYSICS

I can't convey with gestures.
My fingers cannot penetrate, nor can I
magnetize myself.

Understand:
this is not sexual or emotional
but electrical, the path birds take, cellular,

expressed in direction of flight,
following magnetic fields. My fingers want
to practice this flight in you.

LOVE LETTER

Like stationery, crisply
folded, I'm angular, rigid.

You unfold the length
of my body, hold me open

at the hinge of my hips,
a letter, deep in your pocket.

NORTHERN LIGHTS

I understand intrusions: charged
particles, colliding with atmosphere.

Still, I'm thinking of your hair,
how the color, I am certain,

moves in the slowest length,
the slowest calm.

SUMMER

You leaned
your sunburned back, bare

as the neighborhood boys',
against the splintered railing.

The bridge curved above
the water, creaked under your feet.

You hadn't yet been told
to put on your shirt.

LATE AUTUMN

I know your sister worries.
She thinks my illness will make

a nurse out of you,
that I have nothing

to give. It's true
I suffer. You are certain

this will pass.

Today we take the train
north. I nudge you to look out

as rows of houses undulate
against the changing landscape.

THE CROWS KEEP AWAY FROM THE HOUSE

They watch from the edge of the field
as I fill the feeder with seeds,

then retreat to the back porch.
It's Monday. I haven't written in months.

My lover, still warm with sleep
and worry works in the next room.

Each evening we sit on the front porch.
While birds forage, we drink coffee,

watch the moon rise. We look for Hale-Bopp
just above the back pasture.

HOME

You imagine the grist mill before
Hugo swept the wheel downstream,

how it once churned and channeled,
relentlessly working the water,

powering handmade machinery,
sieves and chutes, the red grinding

box. You think about the miller,
the orders piling up, penciled

on the plastered-over beams behind
our cornflower blue living room walls.

UPPER RIGHT

MY MOUTH IS PENITENT

I try to appear as casual
as the woman beside me

at the bar, the one whose black
suit I've been hanging onto

all evening. I'm afraid
of conversations I will never have:

I would tell her I want
to kiss her, but my mouth

is full of winter, dead leaves
and clattering branches.

There is nothing lush
between my lips. I dream

my teeth crumble into my hands.
I should tell her I'm afraid

of kissing, but she won't
believe me. Instead,

I read her lips. Watch her
tongue lick her finger,

turning page after page
of my biography.

WARM BREAD

Like a question you have
to go to the kitchen to find,
no words, only:

the smell of fresh bread
your lover just baked.
These are the answers:

curled up spoon-style
against her prickly backbone.
Your breasts press

flat against her skin. You want
to cut the cord and float
with her in your arms.

My Lover Works Like a Ghost

Cold and quiet,
she doesn't speak.

Light sneaks out
from the space below

the door, streaks
the hallway floor.

WAKING FROM A DREAM

Your alarm clock is merciless
and even if you had a mother
to wake you, it would be
mechanical: another dream
of running. You wake up with
a charley horse, knowing you
have traveled some distance.

GETTING THERE

We had been lovers one month shy
of a year when we decided to leave

the city. What you gave up for me:
anonymity, your sense of safety.

The day we decided to move,
you planned our route, traced

your finger along the Appalachian
outline. You pointed to Mt. Mitchell,

informed me of its altitude: *6,684 ft.,*
the highest peak east of the Mississippi.

You said we should take our time
getting there, study the geography,

document the changing landscape,
the rise and fall of elevation.

The topography between us:
here and now; then and there.

MY LOVER SEARCHES FOR THE RENTAL CAR

It's dark in the parking garage.
I wait on the curb while you

search. Your fingers trail each car
like Braille. You come back empty-

handed, lean to kiss me. My chin
inches forward, my eyes close

the instant my lips brush yours—
a reflex— as if only the blind can kiss.

YOU SAY YOU FEEL SAFER LOCKED UP

Our first year on the farm
I wouldn't let you go

to the grocery store alone.
I stopped whatever I was doing,

clambered into the car
beside you, believed

my presence could protect you.
Now, when you drive away

to teach men in the max facility
down the mountain,

I wonder if the state trooper
idling on the overpass ramp

will catch you in his speed trap.
Will he notice your license

marked female, your boy
body in the driver's seat?

I beg you to obey the rules:
traffic signs, speed limits.

What I really mean:
don't call attention to yourself—

as if you could be visible
only to me, at night,

when the world softens
and blurs.

MY MARRIAGE

We each have our sides.
Six years now without

a license. I could
leave easily. Walk

out the door, out
of our childless lives.

Nothing holds me to my side
of the bed, my back

to the wall. I cup
you in my curled body,

murmur under my breath
yes, I do, take you, choose you

vows we speak each time
we share an avocado:

you carve out the fruit,
show me the hollow boat.

WHEN YOU DRIVE AWAY

I check double check the locks,
my watch. I count mileage

in minutes, factor potential
delays—78 minutes down

shoulderless roads, through narrow
rows of state-owned machinery:

bulldozers and draglines gouge
the alpine edge while workers

wearing orange safety vests juggle
coffee cups and warning signs.

LOWER LEFT

BENEATH SILENCE

I tiptoe to the kitchen to find
my mother busy making bread.

She hums a song from *Oklahoma*
or *South Pacific*—someplace

miles away from the small square
of sky in my bedroom window.

Miles away from last night's
muffled words I held

my breath to hear but never heard
above my own heartbeat.

They called to each other, my mother
and father, across a canyon.

Long vowels, all I could make out
from my bed. I climbed all night

to the kitchen sink, searching
for the source. This morning,

sunlight filters through the curtains.
A flat patch of light spreads

across the floor, frames
my mother as she cracks an egg

against the skillet and hums
another wordless song.

Prayer for Pillows

Do not beg like the unhinged
mouths of birds. Wait as they wait
the long blind hours.

NOW

You no longer hear
the dense hum of snow.
You divide yourself
all ears against my arms.

I Can Almost Hear What Your Fingers Are Signing

I sleep collecting
your knucklebones:
locked fingers
between us. Your hands
break free, cast
frantic finger-shadows
on my nightgown.

MY LOVER COVERS ME WITH A BLANKET

Right there
on the living room floor
where I have fallen
asleep. She anticipates
the chill of sleeping alone,
but I'm not cold. I radiate
heat like a North Carolina
summer down the mountain.
I drown in the humidity
of my descent.

Unnamed Tree on Fifth Street

It's mid-February when
I'm overcome with the need

to name it. I've searched
field guides, fingered spines

thick as branches,
trying to remember the shape

of its leaves in spring.
All winter I worry

about my memory, my lack
of attention to details:

where, when the last leaf fell
I put my keys.

MY LOVER POUNDS THE BOOKSHELF

With both fists. I don't flinch;
I sit motionless on the edge

of our naked bed. Stripped
sheets, limp with humidity,

hang half out of the laundry
basket at my feet. The tops

of my teeth touch, won't let go
of each other. *I should*

speak. I know I should speak.
Instead, I sit paralyzed by her

outline, the shape of each book
as the shelves shake.

SEEDS

Like my lover's
ringless fingers
unfurl inside me,
relentless birds
break frozen ground.

DOWSER

I press my ear to the earth,
I'm certain I hear water.

I watch rain wash deer tracks
clean away as if they had never

snuck down to the house.
Later, I see my lover's footsteps

leading to the woodpile
slowly collapse under snow.

MIRED

When my work boots stuck,
stubborn in the mud,
I had to leave them standing
empty in the rain-soaked yard.

FOOL QUAIL

I prefer to stand still
and listen to my heartbeat
instead of your voice:

gunshots, sirens.
I know I could fly. I could
leave everything behind.

Restlessness
reverberates in my bones,
makes me pace hallways.

I could leave you effortlessly.

SIR, YOU'LL HAVE TO LEAVE

You walk past her; you pass
women groping for towels,

the steaming showers. Her words
condense in your lungs, steep

inside you. She waves
the cleaner, finger to trigger,

aims at the Exit sign
above the locker room.

LOWER RIGHT

WALKING OUT

The trees bleed
together in the background:

the brightest maples.
We sat underneath

a tree, its trunk split into
two arms ready to take flight.

AFTER THE FUNERAL

As you opened the door and stepped
over the threshold, you could feel
the deep beating of wings at your back.

The red-tailed hawk hurled himself
headlong into the picture window.
You buried him in the garden

before I could see his body, where
three summers ago, Stella stood
on the lawn to say one last goodnight.

You wonder why death follows you,
like the hawk to the front porch,
before you open the door.

WINDOWPANES

I thought I was broken.
The bird threw itself,

suicide at my mother's reflection,
the four quarters of her face.

I learned that glass is liquid.
I thought about my own

body of water, how I see
my father reflected there.

HER DEATH

The day the disoriented hawk
misjudged his prey, one inch
off his mark, collided
with the window. Just like that.

WHAT TO CALL IT

Your hands feel detached,
unable to execute routine

actions. Each task
involves the act of forgetting

simple sequence. First
reach   contact   grasp

the book. Then pull
toward you. All syntax

mangled in translation.
You wonder if you will recover.

.

THEN

I held your ear
with my cupped hand.
Remember this
I must have whispered
before we each moved
deeper into winter.

FLURRIES

Each arm of each flake,
a happenstance radiating
independently,

longing for symmetry.
Precipitation so exact,
you don't question

the origin. *What's wrong?*
Your lover doesn't ask
as if you could stop it.

ACCUMULATION

Snow spirals through the empty
locust branches outside our bedroom

window. I know without looking
she's staring at me as snow falls

steadily. I know without asking
she doesn't want to have sex.

Something is always falling
when we fight. Not really fight—

just two people
on either side of a window.

SUNLIGHT

All summer you were with me.
My face darkened, the light

peach walls glowed when
you entered my room.

You were persistent, kept me up
later each evening, wanted me

each moment to notice.
Sometimes you were too much.

Sometimes I wanted to
turn off the light. Now

I've gotten what I asked for.
You've turned yourself away.

WEATHER REPORT

I would contain you,
take each of your fingers inland,

but winter weather threatens
the road between us.

I wait for you, wondering
Do you want me?

Uncertainty as sudden
as this blizzard,

fogging my vision like windows
from the heat inside.

My Lover Doesn't Touch Me Anymore

I recognize this distance:
no more than our own sides

of the bed and how
you don't move to kiss me.

We have talked of taking other
lovers, but I can't imagine

kissing a new body
or fitting in quite

the same way
and even though I love

many women, it is you
I want to move with wildly.

COVE CREEK

I.
Rain shifts to hurricane. First
Francis, then Ivan on her heels.
We watch the creek darken,
deep brown, pushing itself over
the bridge and through widening
cracks in the retaining wall.

II.
Last night we looked at pictures:
How it once was small, a harmless
trickle outlining the edge of the yard.

III.
Next month the county's bringing
bulldozers and boulders to begin
the work of creek bank restoration.
For six months now, we've tried
to salvage the disintegrating
beams running under our feet:
what's left of our foundation.

MIGRATION

I go miles without
a marker, something to gauge
how far I've come.

Water everywhere:
for days nothing changes.

Acknowledgments

Many thanks to the editors of the following publications, in which these poems appeared, sometimes in earlier versions:

Asheville Poetry Review: "Windowpanes"

Clementine Unbound: "Flurries"

Cold Mountain Review: "Physics"

Eunoia Review: "After the Funeral," "Beneath Silence," "Her Mother Holds the Cup Like a Weapon," "Sunlight"

One Art: a journal of poetry: "Late Autumn"

Trouvaille Review: "Unnamed Tree on Fifth Street"

Voices from the Attic: "Your Sister Brings Me an Orchard"

ABOUT THE AUTHOR

Elizabeth Wilson is an aspiring tap dancer, chronic illness advocate, and Rising Voices of Narcolepsy speaker, living with her partner and son in the North Carolina mountains. She is the winner of the 2021 Patricia Dobler Poetry Award and received her MFA from Hunter College.

HEADMISTRESS PRESS BOOKS

Windowpanes - Elizabeth Wilson
Everything We Need - Laura Foley
Tender, Tender - Jessica Jewell
A Trickle of Bloom Becomes You - Jen Rouse
Cyborg Sister - Jackie Craven
Demoted Planet - Katherine Fallon
Earlier Households - Bonnie J. Morris
The Things We Bring with Us: Travel Poems - S.G. Huerta
The Water Between Us - Gillian Ebersole
Discomfort - Sarah Caulfield
The History of a Voice - Jessica Jopp
I Wish My Father - Lesléa Newman
Tender Age - Luiza Flynn-Goodlett
Low-water's Edge - Jean A. Kingsley
Routine Bloodwork - Colleen McKee
Queer Hagiographies - Audra Puchalski
Why I Never Finished My Dissertation - Laura Foley
The Princess of Pain - Carolyn Gage & Sudie Rakusin
Seed - Janice Gould
Riding with Anne Sexton - Jen Rouse
Spoiled Meat - Nicole Santalucia
Cake - Jen Rouse
The Salt and the Song - Virginia Petrucci
mad girl's crush tweet - summer jade leavitt
Saturn coming out of its Retrograde - Briana Roldan
i am this girl - gina marie bernard
Week/End - Sarah Duncan
My Girl's Green Jacket - Mary Meriam
Nuts in Nutland - Mary Meriam & Hannah Barrett
Lovely - Lesléa Newman
Teeth & Teeth - Robin Reagler
How Distant the City - Freesia McKee
Shopgirls - Marissa Higgins

Riddle - Diane Fortney
When She Woke She Was an Open Field - Hilary Brown
A Crown of Violets - Renée Vivien tr. Samantha Pious
Fireworks in the Graveyard - Joy Ladin
Social Dance - Carolyn Boll
The Force of Gratitude - Janice Gould
Spine - Sarah Caulfield
I Wore the Only Garden I've Ever Grown - Kathryn Leland
Diatribe from the Library - Farrell Greenwald Brenner
Blind Girl Grunt - Constance Merritt
Acid and Tender - Jen Rouse
Beautiful Machinery - Wendy DeGroat
Odd Mercy - Gail Thomas
The Great Scissor Hunt - Jessica K. Hylton
A Bracelet of Honeybees - Lynn Strongin
Whirlwind @ Lesbos - Risa Denenberg
The Body's Alphabet - Ann Tweedy
First name Barbie last name Doll - Maureen Bocka
Heaven to Me - Abe Louise Young
Sticky - Carter Steinmann
Tiger Laughs When You Push - Ruth Lehrer
Night Ringing - Laura Foley
Paper Cranes - Dinah Dietrich
On Loving a Saudi Girl - Carina Yun
The Burn Poems - Lynn Strongin
I Carry My Mother - Lesléa Newman
Distant Music - Joan Annsfire
The Awful Suicidal Swans - Flower Conroy
Joy Street - Laura Foley
Chiaroscuro Kisses - G.L. Morrison
The Lillian Trilogy - Mary Meriam
Lady of the Moon - Amy Lowell, Lillian Faderman, Mary Meriam
Irresistible Sonnets - ed. Mary Meriam
Lavender Review - ed. Mary Meriam

Made in the USA
Columbia, SC
12 September 2024

41507516R00039